# Worlingworth
# Past and Present

## IN PHOTOGRAPHS

# Volume 2

*Gloria. Rosemary Ingate*

Compiled by
Geoffrey Robinson
Rosemary Ingate

A second volume of old photographs of
Worlingworth and the surrounding parishes

The publication of this book and half of the proceeds from its sale will be used to help in financing improvements to Worlingworth Community Centre.

Compiled, edited and published by the Worlingworth Local History Group.

ISBN 978-0-9572292-2-8

Printed in Great Britain by The Lavenham Press Limited.
First published in 2016

# Contents

# FOREWORD

After the success of the first Worlingworth book launched for the Queen's Diamond Jubilee in 2012, it seems fitting that in the year we celebrate the Queen's 90th birthday, another book of photographs from Worlingworth and beyond is published.

As Lady Henniker said in her Foreword last time "change is so fast today; there is not enough time to understand who we are or where we have come from or why things are as they are. We are overwhelmed with information which we don't know what to do with, so it is good to spend a little time looking at the past, looking about us; perhaps seeing what our forbears saw or what is left of their world."

We travel at such a pace in 2016 that the chance to view how our community has grown and changed through the photography of bygone times give us all a sense of place. Over decades, buildings have seen families come and go under different ownership yet the structures have survived the passage of time. Whether a recent arrival to Suffolk or a family with long links, we are all custodians of the properties in our villages during our occupation and the chance to look back at the previous generations is very heart-warming.

This is another fascinating opportunity to explore the past and many congratulations to all those who have spent such a lot of time collating and putting together "Worlingworth Past and Present In Photographs Volume Two."

Matthew Hicks
Suffolk County Councillor

# INTRODUCTION

History, especially parish history, is a very deep and convoluted subject with many interwoven layers. It can encompass great national events of celebration right down to the family baptism or the departure of a familiar face from the community. It is important to recognise that the images of the past, whether from the 1890s or the 1980s, are equally relevant in telling us something about our heritage.

People used to say that "nothing ever happened in Worlingworth" but this could not be further from the truth. Take a look at what happened in 2012. We celebrated the Diamond Jubilee in fine style and we enjoyed another traditional village fete; we walked around a beautiful wildflower meadow and enjoyed the church flower festival. We also enjoyed a "Safari Supper" with a theme based on the TV comedy series "Allo Allo" and we launched the first Worlingworth book of photographs. Those events were only what you might call "the major events of the year".

Worlingworth was once described by a 19th century antiquarian as being "far removed from civilisation". But when Worlingworth celebrates, it is the centre of the earth.

This second book of photographs about Worlingworth and its surroundings should be considered as a follow up to the first volume which was published in 2012. Whereas the first volume was divided into three subject areas, we have set out this second book in a roughly chronological order and we have included some delightful images from neighbouring parishes on the basis that they might never otherwise be published.

I hope that you, the reader, will find much to enjoy in this second book. It has again been rewarding to put this collection of images together and one hopes that both volumes will sit well together on your book shelf.

Geoffrey Robinson
August 2016

1. This is a portrait of John Henniker-Major, the 4th Lord Henniker. He succeeded his father John Minet Henniker-Major to the estates and titles in 1832 and served as an MP for East Suffolk before being created a Baron in 1866. He married Lady Anna Kerrison, daughter of Sir Edward Kerrison of Brome Hall and Oakley Park. They had five children, the eldest son John succeeding to the estates and titles on his father's death in 1870. A stained glass window was erected by public subscription in Worlingworth church to his memory.

2. The marriage of John Henniker-Major and Lady Anna Kerrison was a great event and it brought together two of the most important families in the district. The marriage took place at Hoxne church on January 5th 1837 and the Henniker estates and their tenantry would have been *en fete*. Sadly, Lord Henniker's mother, Mary, the Dowager Lady Henniker died five days later at Major House (later to be named Thornham Hall).

3. The 5th Lord Henniker (pictured above) presided over landholdings in Suffolk amounting to over 30,000 acres in the 1870s. Thornham Hall and its splendid estate was in its heyday and was a popular destination for London society, with its summer balls and its weekend shooting parties. Regular visitors included the Prince of Wales and a number of Indian princes such as Freddie Duleep Singh. (Photo credit—Suffolk Records Office SRO)

4. This genteel young lady would become an important part of the social life of the parish in the mid 20th century. Ethel Elizabeth Henniker-Major is portrayed here, possibly for a 21st birthday photograph in the Isle of Man in 1895. Her father, the 5th Lord Henniker, had been appointed Governor of the Isle of Man in that year. Ethel married the Reverend George Wilkes in 1920. (Photo credit SRO)

5. If you were one of Lord Henniker's tenant farmers in the Worlingworth of the 1870s, you would have known the gentleman pictured above. William Henry Preston (1832-1901) was the land agent for the Henniker Worlingworth estates. William was the second son of Henry Preston of Grove Farm and a half-brother to Alfred Preston, the auctioneer.

6. William H. Preston's younger brother Arthur emigrated to Australia in the 1860s and took another brother, Harry, with him. Pictured is Arthur with his wife and their seven children. They settled in Queensland where descendants live to this day.

7. Anna Maria Preston was William and Arthur Preston's younger sister. All three siblings were baptised at Worlingworth in the 1830s and grew up at the Grove Farm. Anna Maria was betrothed to William Aldous of Bedfield Hall and went to live there after her marriage. Her husband died young and she took over the management of the farm. Some fragments of her diaries survive—she was a religious woman and she looks quite severe in this image from the 1880s.

8. A wonderful portrait of Richard Tissington who was the schoolmaster at the old Schoolroom from 1860 until 1869. He succeeded his brother Silvester, who was fatally injured in an accident at Stradbroke in the summer of 1860. Richard eventually married his brother's widow Betsy, who was a granddaughter of the parish clerk John Clayton.

9. and 10. Elizabeth Tissington was the first born child of Silvester and Betsy Tissington. She was born in 1855 and was therefore only five years old when her father died. Silvester was a very popular and likeable master of the Free School from 1851 until his death.

Frederick Richard Tissington was the first born child of Richard and Betsy in the summer of 1869. His birth was registered in Manchester, suggesting that the couple had already left the parish. By September 1869, John and Jane Holland had been appointed as schoolmaster and schoolmistress of the old School.

11. Jonathan Pettit was born and bred in Worlingworth in 1814. He and his wife Crystal brought up their family at Valley Farm Cottage on New Road in the 1840s. They shared this cottage with another family. Jonathan took the momentous decision to emigrate in 1851 and the family sailed for Australia that winter. They arrived in Sydney on January 4th 1852. Jonathan reputedly had just a shilling in his pocket. Initially he worked as a gardener for people but eventually he was able to buy some land in Kew, a suburb of Melbourne. When he retired in the 1880s, he was a market gardener of some repute and he sold a parcel of his land for £5,000 to fund his well-deserved retirement.

12. Frances Pettit, born in 1833, was one of seven children to Jonathan and Crystal. She was a domestic servant for a farmer in Brundish before the epic journey to Australia, where she married and had thirteen children of her own.

13. This image of St. Mary's church was one of a series of early 20th century postcards. Note the weather-vane on the top of the flagpole on the church tower.

14. Chandos Farm on Tannington Road was a farm of about 100 acres, which belonged to the Henniker estate. Robert Plant is pictured standing with his wife Mary, who was blind, and their daughter. This very early photograph dates from the 1860s.

15. The Worlingworth Shop and Post Office, managed by the Clarke family for many years, was once known as Vine House. Looking at this image, one can understand why!

16. This close-up of a John Self postcard shows some of the carts and wagons that were repaired or being repaired by the village blacksmith and wheelwright at the Forge next to St. Mary's church. Note the footpath on the right which has now disappeared.

17. Old Ivy Cottage (now White Cottage) on Shop Street is pictured here in about 1908 with its covering of ivy. Matilda Newson and her children, Bessie and Stephen, are stood by the roadside.

18. Here is Cross Cottage near the Swan Inn with Mrs. Eliza Chapman standing outside. The chimney on the right looks a little unstable!

19. Many of the older images of Worlingworth capture the luxuriant nature of the gardens and hedgerows. This is Willow Farm on Shop Street.

20. When the Maltings was built in the 18th century, a small cottage was erected as living accommodation for the malster and the cottage still stands today, virtually unchanged from so many years ago.

21. Stanway Green Farm was one of the principal Henniker farms in Worlingworth. For many years it was in the tenancy of the Spurlings. William Spurling was gamekeeper in the early 1800s. The family emigrated to Australia in 1852 where descendants live today. These Spurlings were a different family to the 20th century tenants of the Crown pub.

22. Oak Tree Farm on Fingal Street was a smallholding of between 18 and 25 acres. This 19th century view looks onto the front barns with the house in the background. On the right, Elizabeth Copping stands next to her horse and cart.

23. This is Martin Peter Cracknell and Elizabeth Copping. Martin was her brother-in-law. This photograph may have been taken before Elizabeth moved away from Worlingworth in about 1875. In October the previous year, her husband Joseph had fatally shot himself in the head with his gun. Elizabeth appears to be wearing her mourning apparel.

24. This study of Elizabeth Copping captures her quiet dignity following the distressing events of 1874. After her husband's suicide, she and her six children left Oak Tree Farm and they went to live with her brother Alfred Betts in London. Elizabeth was born at the brickworks at Athelington which the Betts family ran as a business for over 40 years.

25, 26 and 27. William and Anna Maria Cornish (above). William was a chimney sweep who lived on Fingal Street throughout most of the Victorian era. In the 1850s, William served a sentence of three months hard labour for "highway robbery". Their daughter Bertha (pictured below right with her own daughter Dora) married John Stammers who sold "fowls, fish and fruit" in Bedfield.

28 and 29. Here we have two very old images. Above are a group of locals standing in the front yard of the Crown beerhouse on Fingal Street. (Photo credit SRO.) Below the Knights family of Horham in an image from about 1900. Thomas Knights was a licensed hawker and his shop was situated close to the Eight Bells public house on The Street.

30. Another shop in Horham, still standing today, is the old Horham Post Office of the 1890s. The dilapidated section was subsequently demolished. This photograph was taken from the Horham-Redlingfield road. The church and the old Dragon Inn are to the left of this view.

31. A photographer has returned a few years later to record the same view of the post office building from the Redlingfield road.

32. Further along from the post office and shop is the Horham main street. This photograph was taken from the churchyard looking west with the Horham windmill in the background.

33. Down a short drive on the road back to Worlingworth is the Horham Baptist Chapel. This striking building replaced the original chapel in 1859 and it has been a place of worship for over two hundred years.

34. This is the original farmhouse of Honeypots Farm on New Road. Most of this house was demolished when a new house was built circa 1907. Past residents of this house would have been John Blomfield, a popular churchwarden of the mid 19th century, and William Godbold, who left a charitable bequest to the parish in his will of 1698.

35. Charles and Rosa Blomfield lived at Carters Farm in the 1890s. Charles was a grandson of John Blomfield, the eminent Victorian churchwarden and he spent some of his childhood living in the Honeypots farmhouse pictured above.

36 and 37. Tannington Hall (above) was the home of members of the Ray family for most of the 19th century, along with Tannington Place (below) and the Red House. The Ray family wealth stemmed from the sale of butter, malt, spirits and drapery from their shop and maltings on Shop Street in Worlingworth and from their property investments in the district and abroad.

38. Tannington Street near the church in about 1900. It is somehow difficult to imagine this scene existing now. Nothing in this picture remains—just a few car parking spaces for the church and a more modern house called Little Braiseworth. (Photo credit SRO)

39. Here is a lovely old image of Bedingfield Hall, some parts of which date back to the 15th century.

40. White Hall Farm used to be called Green Farm because of its proximity to Worlingworth Green. Here we see Henry Maybury carrying out some repairs on the chimney.

41. Mill Farm in the 1930s and thatched. The hedge and gate may have originally marked the boundary between the farm and the common land known as Worlingworth Green. This common land was enclosed by Order of Parliament in 1832.

42. Miss Emma Clayton, nursemaid to the infants at the Rectory in 1895. Emma was the eldest surviving daughter of James Clayton, who for forty-seven years, was the coachman and faithful servant to the Reverend Frederic French. Emma was also the mother of Bruce and Clayton Hill.

43. In 1881, John Clayton, son of Isaac Clayton, pictured opposite, married Eliza Larter at the parish church in 1881 and this photograph may have been taken as a memento of the occasion. The image is not in good condition but it conveys something about the fashions of that period and for the descendants, it is a valuable image of their heritage. The Clayton family were an important part of the Worlingworth gene-pool. (John's grandfather had 43 grandchildren when he died in 1872.)

44. Isaac Clayton, seated on the left, was Emma Clayton's great uncle and this photo was taken in about 1880. Three of Isaac's daughters, Anne, Hannah and Emma married three brothers James, Henry and William Simpson. Perhaps the three couples are pictured here.

45. In 1899, the Caravan Mission to Village Children from Pettaugh visited the school.

46. Revivalism and evangelism were two different but intertwined religious movements of the 19th century. They were evolving popular alternatives to the staid, formal Church of England. The Caravan Mission to Village Children was a local movement offering open-air Christian learning, singing and Bible reading to village school children. James Cutting of Abbots Hall, Pettaugh became a convert and helped drive the first caravan through the villages of Suffolk.

47. Perhaps it is of significance that the headmaster Mr. Alfred Boocock is absent from the photograph although Mrs. Jane Holland, the infants mistress and widow of John Holland is pictured on the extreme right. Many of these schoolchildren are also pictured in some of the class photographs of the period.

48. A lovely family portrait of Hubert Holland, his wife Edith and their children. Hubert was a son of John Holland, the Worlingworth schoolmaster and Edith was the daughter of William Aldous and Anna Maria Preston of Bedfield Hall. Hubert became Mayor of Ipswich in the 1930s. This image dates from about 1910.

49. This postcard was sent from Eye to Dolly Tate at Stradbroke Rectory in 1910. The gentleman in the coat and hat is almost certainly Frederick W. French J.P., the eldest son of Rev. Frederic French. His wife Minna is in the back of the car. The car is an unknown custom-built model and the registration number is obscured.

50. David Collins, our renowned bellringer, was legendary for his habit of walking everywhere. He began ringing aged 14 and once walked the 13 miles to Redenhall where 114 ringers were present, so he just turned around and left without a ring.

51. Hidden away behind a high hedge on Swan Road is Grange Farm, the venue of the first Cart Colt Show in 1879. Robert and Frances (Fanny) Chambers stand outside.

52. Robert Chambers was a dealer in livestock of some reputation in the district. He often hosted the Easton Harriers hunt and was a keen member of the Swan Bowls team.

53. Robert's wife was born Fanny Curtis (pictured above) and her first husband George Chapman, the Bedfield grocer, died suddenly at the age of 34. They had three children, the eldest daughter being Clara Chapman. Fanny married Robert Chambers in 1875 and they moved from the Bedfield shop to Grange Farm. On the death of her mother and stepfather in 1922, Clara became a very wealthy spinster.

54. Bull's Hall in Bedfield has been occupied by the Steel family for over 100 years. Arthur Steel came from Wyverstone and married local girl Dinah Chapman in 1887. Dinah was Clara Chapman's sister. Arthur (seated) lost an arm in an accident on the farm shortly after this picture was taken in 1912.

55. From left to right Dick, Jack on the donkey and Barney Steel in the farmyard during the First World War years.

56. Patty Steel, a daughter of Arthur and Dinah, was an aspiring young woman who had passed her examinations and become an assistant teacher at Worlingworth school. By all accounts, she was destined for a very good career in the teaching profession. In early February 1913, she was excused her duties after complaining of being unwell and she returned home. The doctor diagnosed a brain affliction and there was nothing that could be done for her. Within a week she had died, probably of a brain tumour. She was just 21 years old.

57. This is a portrait picture of Walter Cecil Steel, otherwise known as Barney, that was taken in about 1918. One of the fields belonging to the Steel family was used as an emergency landing strip for the Royal Flying Corps during the First World War.

58. These young boys do not look comfortable in front of the camera tripod. Tom and Clayton Hill, who were about three and four years old at the time (1913), were two of Emma Clayton's sons, growing up in Worlingworth during and after the First World War. Clayton is pictured later in this book with the Rev. Bill Donnan.

59. This old lady was purportedly a relative of the late David Feaverearyear but her name is something of a mystery. Nevertheless she looks very happy—perhaps she has just taken a scrumptious fruit pie out of the oven!

60. David and Louisa Feaverearyear with their three daughters, Kate, Bessie and Agnes in front of their home Yew Tree Farm, Fingal Street in about 1908.

61. The three girls are a little older in this studio portrait.

62. Rose Finbow and her daughter Kate who would grow up to marry Walter "Font" Whatling. Kate's two brothers, Harry and George, both served their country during the First World War. They are pictured later in this book.

63. This image came to our notice after the publication of the book "Worlingworth's Fallen" in 2014. William James Blaxall was just 18 years old when he enlisted in the Suffolk Regiment in 1915. He died in Rouen Hospital in February 1917.

*Father of Gerald Harry + V*

64. A family photograph taken in the early 1910s of Arthur and Elizabeth Hawes and their children. They resided at Green Farm on Southolt Green. Stanley (back row centre) was killed during the War and is commemorated on the Southolt war memorial.

65. In 1915 outside Worlingworth School, the Local Defence Volunteers were caught on camera for posterity. William Leggett, churchwarden, is third from the right in the back row. Most of these men and boys are unidentified.

66. Pictured here on the left is Private Stanley Hawes of the 4th Suffolks. Stanley lost his life at High Wood on August 18th 1916 during the Somme Offensive. The soldier on the right may be one of the Stearne brothers, three of whom also gave their lives for their country during the Great War.

67. Most of our archive of school photographs were shown in the first Worlingworth book. This recently acquired pair of images came from a direct descendant of Frederick Perry, schoolmaster. This 1912 image of the juniors shows Patty Steel, assistant teacher on the left.

68. In 1913, Worlingworth School Group 2 with Miss Harvey and headmaster Perry. At this time, extensive improvements were made to the school buildings and an infants room was built.

69. The school garden, school house and Mr. and Mrs. Perry with son Haldon in about 1913.

70. Much later in the decade, in about 1918, this small group photograph of pupils was taken at the back of the school house. Miss Amy McLenaghan (left) was the first woman to be appointed head before she decided to emigrate to New Zealand. The boy on the left of the top row looks like Clayton Hill.

71. This photograph of an unnamed girl was taken by the old Guildhall cottages opposite the church. The Guildhall was built in about 1575, according to the leasehold. It was once the parish poorhouse and was converted into dwellings for six families in 1836.

72. As a contrast to the picture opposite, in 1912 we find the Lings of Valley Farm having a family photograph taken. From L to R are little Samuel, Ellen, mother Agnes, baby Frederick and William Francis Ling.

73. Alfred Preston of Grove Farm, Shop Street, was a well-known auctioneer and land agent. He was also for many years secretary of the Suffolk Horse Society and he was one of the first pupils at Framlingham College. Here he is seen conducting a sale of livestock for the Red Cross in about 1915. He stands in his own motor car.

74. Alfred Preston's office on Market Hill in Framlingham can be seen on the left of this image and is now the location of Victoria's bookshop next to "Panorama".

Page 58

75. Bedfield war memorial unveiled in April 1920. Many faces look on but we do not know any of their names, except for the priest, the Reverend W.T. Pratt.

76. In this image, we know the "who" but not the "where" or the "when". We will never know for sure, but a young-looking Ethel and Reverend George Wilkes are enjoying a promenade together. This could be a south coast resort such as Torquay and it could be their honeymoon in 1926.

77. Now we see some of the fashions in wedding apparel in the 1920s. This is the wedding of Lilian Beecroft and Harold Sturgeon in 1925.

78. Lilian Beecroft's brother Herbert married Daisy Whatling just months before her own wedding. Short trouser legs must have been all the fashion in those days.

79. Herbert and Daisy were Noel Beecroft's parents. In this photograph, Herbert is stood on the path leading to the front door of his parents home at the Willow Farm Cottages opposite the Swan Inn.

80. Here is a wedding photograph of Maurice Chapman and Elsie Smith outside Worlingworth church in 1927.

81 and 82. Contrasting images. Two groups of unidentified children believed to date from the 1920s. The three girls in the top image are playing near the New School whilst the lower image shows the children in front of the Guildhall cottages.

83. An opportunity was taken to photograph the Rumsey children at the School in 1922. Here are Gordon Rumsey and his sisters Kathleen, Marjorie and Dorothy. It makes for an interesting comparison to see these groups of children and the clothes that they wore.

84. Norton Smith won the Framlingham Bowls Tournament in 1926 and here he sits with his trophies. Norton was just 20 years old at the time. In 1934, he married Kathleen Wright and by 1940 he was the landlord of the Swan Inn.

85 and 86. Sam Catling will always be associated with the harness makers and saddlers shop opposite the church. He was also Captain of the Worlingworth Fire Engine team. His saddlers shop was renowned as a meeting place for news, gossip and discussion for the old stalwarts of the village. Here he is pictured with his wife Kate. One of their sons was Russell John Catling who wrote of his memories of Worlingworth in the 1930s.

87. Emma Kate Catling was a cultured woman. Strictly religious, she played the piano to her children, smoked with a cigarette holder and was a wonderful letter writer. She was equally superstitious and taught all her children the country ways. Her hobby was flower gardening.

88. Here Mr. Catling stands outside his shop with his granddaughter Elizabeth. Amongst his own recollections, Sam told us of the year of the fete when Rev. French was pulled into the moat of the Guildhall during a tug of war.

89, 90 and 91. The Worlingworth Mill (above) was completely dismantled in about 1950, having served the parish since 1862. It had been redundant for a number of years. The roundhouse of an older mill still survives and is pictured bottom right. Wind power would be replaced by steam power in later years.

During the First World War, the travelling fan-tail was painted in the patriotic colours of red, white and blue. In 1921, the last of the Moultons, Thomas, passed away and the mill, the cottage and its premises were subsequently operated by the Greenard family.

Pictured above right are William Greenard (d. 1941) and his son Russell. This photograph can be dated to the 1930s. Another son David married Ethel Hobson in 1945 and Ethel came to Worlingworth, a town girl not particularly familiar with country ways. However she lived in the Mill Cottage for much of the rest of her life. A particularly vivid memory she recounted was of her first visit to the privy which she shared with a large rodent!

92. These two photographs show father Harry Mayhew and son Walter at Wood Farm, the home of Edwin Preston and then Daisy Wolton. Edwin and Daisy showed their Suffolk Punch horses regularly at the annual Framlingham Horse Show.

93. Harry Mayhew was a son of Walter and Kate Mayhew of New Town, Worlingworth. He and his wife Sally and their large family lived at Moss Farm on the Tannington Road.

94. This mid-1930s image brings together a number of well-known youthful faces. From left to right, Betty Spinner, Esme Bridges, Betty Crowe, Brenda Crowe, Dora Beecroft, Audrey Crowe and Jean Hambling with Eric Smith and Maisie Crowe sat at the front.

95. David Bridges and his wife Emma displaying the fruits of their cottage gardening.

On October 10th 1940, a tragic event occurred in Fingal Street which shocked the parish and the surrounding district. An unexploded German bomb went off, claiming the lives of five members of No. 4 Bomb Disposal Section, Royal Engineers and our village bobby, P.C. Ernest Whiting.
We remember them all here.

96. Our previous book featured the photograph opposite, which we were informed was of P.C. Ernest Whiting. Unfortunately this was not the case and we were unable to correct the error at the time, the book having already been printed. We most sincerely apologise for this mistake but we are now able to put the record straight and finally publish a photograph of Ernest Whiting, provided by his family.

97. We now believe that this is one of the five Royal Engineers who lost their lives on that day. Research has not been able to identify him but we know the names of those five other men:

Thomas P. Carter aged 35 and buried at Goole Cemetery
Harry Edwards aged 39 and buried at Wisbech Mt Pleasant Cemetery
Thomas Renz aged 33 and buried at Edinburgh Rosebank Cemetery
George W. Simpson aged 33 and buried in Gorleston Cemetery
Frank B. Wooldridge aged 21 and interred at Birmingham Cemetery
May they all rest in eternal peace.

98. Taken in the front garden of the police house on Fingal Street in 1941, a group of girls—back row (l to r) Maisie Crowe, Jean Whiting, Stephanie Minor, kneeling are Hazel Crowe, Marian Whiting and the youngest Patricia Whiting.

99. Threshing under steam power at Patrick Lane during the winter in the early 1940s. Jack Lawes was in charge of the threshing tackle.

100. Harry Finbow Senior in pensive mood in 1945. His two sons served in the First World War and both survived. Harry was a horseman for much of his life.

101. Sam Catling and three of his sisters stand behind their elderly parents, Charles and Barbara Catling. Family pictures such as this usually meant an important event—this might have been their golden wedding anniversary in 1945.

102. In the late 40s, young Ray Mayhew and Charlie Abbott used to climb up the steps and ladders to the top of the church tower, with the permission of the Reverend Wilkes!

103. The Church Road council houses were built just after the war and here some ladies relax in the front garden of one of those houses. .

104. To the right: Margaret Beecroft, Sheila and Edna Mayhew and Janet Gobbitt having a great time on an outing to Clacton in 1949.

105. Gerald Hawes and Ted Mayhew were a little distance away from Worlingworth in June 1952. They were to be found on the back of a camel in Egypt as they took a break during their National Service. They were both serving with the R.A.F.

106. The cat looks friendly enough. Lionel "Digger" Turnbull and his wife Margaret do not seem to be too worried in this photograph taken on their honeymoon in Germany in 1952 where Digger was stationed. On setting up home in Worlingworth, Margaret taught at the Primary School.

107. A long "mixed" train carrying goods and passengers, leaving Worlingworth station for Laxfield on the Mid-Suffolk Light Railway.

108. The Worlingworth football team in the 1950s. Back Row (l to r): Ivan Stannard, Dick Mayhew, Geoff Jay, Gordon Stannard, Dennis Jay and John Farrington. Front row: Noel Beecroft, Ray Watts, Gerald Hawes, Gordon Jay and Jimmy Gobbitt.

109. Worlingworth Football Club were the winners of the Leiston Football League in the 1950s. In the back row are from left to right Geoff Jay, Dennis Jay, Gerald Hawes, Joe Nightingale, Brian Soames and John Farrington whilst the front row from left to right are John Gobbitt, Arthur Rose, Gordon Jay, Ned Cuthbert and Ray Mayhew.

110. The football team are enjoying their annual club dinner in the convivial surroundings of the Worlingworth Swan. From left to right are Ellis Farrington, Arthur Rose, Gordon Jay, Geoff Jay, Charlie Wright and Gerald Hawes.

111. In 1952, Geoff Weavers leads the horse as Dick and George Ingate begin their farm working life. Dick was only 10 years old and George was 12.

112. Dick, Nora and George Ingate are all smiles on the driveway at Patrick Lane Farm.

113. Two young men continuing their education at the Suffolk Show at Shrubland Park in June 1952. Dick and George Ingate are accompanied by their father Alfred and Geoff Weavers.

114. Here are four photographs taken when the last train on the Mid-Suffolk Light Railway came through Worlingworth in July 1952.

115. Clearly, local residents wanted to dress up lavishly in order to commemorate the demise of their local train. Note the Worlingworth mill in the background.

116. Tom Hambling, station master, always had a smile for the camera—even on such a sad day as the closing of the railway.

117. The train is packed full and the platform has a number of well-wishers ready to wave the train on to Laxfield. In the first Worlingworth book, a photograph was taken looking at the rear of the train.

118. A Bank Holiday outing to Great Yarmouth in the 1950s. Pictured are Sandra Spurling, Mrs Catling and her daughter Joyce and behind are John Smith with his mother Edna.

119. The Southolt Plough Darts Club Annual Outing in 1955 was recorded for posterity with this splendid photograph. Many names are given in the appendices at the back of the book.

120. On an similar 1950s outing, standing in front of the motor coach are Rena Spurling, George Finbow, one-time village postman, and Dolly Bridges.

121. Worlingworth Juniors football team in the early 1950s. Their names are given in the appendices at the back of the book.

122. The marriage of Stephen Rodwell and Janet Gobbitt in 1956 was officiated by the Reverend Norman Southgate who was rector here in Worlingworth from 1956 to 1961. He was succeeded as rector by the Reverend William Donnan.

123. Another 1956 wedding took place at Horham Baptist Chapel between Reggie Catling and Eileen Farrow. Here are the happy couple with their bridesmaids, Jean Batell and Reggie's younger sister Joyce Catling.

124. Outside the Worlingworth Crown, Harry and Rena Spurling pose with their new-born baby boy Johnny. The Spurlings ran the Worlingworth Crown from 1952 and 1965. One of the benefits of being a patron of the Crown was the annual outing to a seaside resort such as Great Yarmouth.

125. Here is an interesting study of Riley George Whatling, master thatcher, with his wife Emma and Mrs. Agnes Spinner (kneeling) in the garden of 2 Mill Road in the late 1950s. Agnes is pictured earlier in the book with her parents and sisters.

126. Kye Lawes (left) brought the threshing tackle to Green Farm, Southolt during the early 1960s for his last threshing season. Standing next to him is Alfred Henry Ingate.

127. Another photograph of threshing at Green Farm, Southolt with Dick Ingate driving.

Page 96

128. Members of the Worlingworth Royal British Legion Women's Section in 1970 receiving Poppy Day Collection Certificates of Appreciation from the Branch President, Mrs. Monica Gooch. Pictured with Mrs Gooch are Bessie Baldry (Bedfield), Elsie Abbott (Worlingworth) and Maudie Hart (Tannington).

129. Stephen Horvath (left) with a friend outside the Crown Inn, Framlingham.

130. Reverend William Donnan and his wife Joyce came to Worlingworth in 1961. This earlier photograph probably dates to the 1950s.

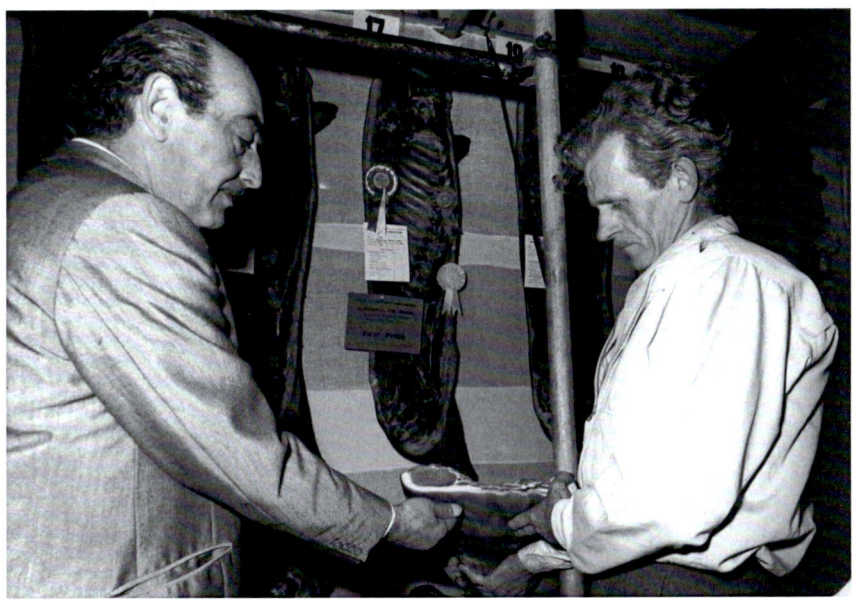

131. Stephen Horvath (left) and Karl Spandl were from Eastern Europe and they became good friends after Karl was given a job on the farm at Stanway Green. After Mr. Horvath died, Spandl tended his grave every year until he himself died at the graveside in 1988.

132. Karl Spandl was livestock manager for Horvath Farms and he won a number of prizes for his skill in the breeding and rearing of their pigs.

133. Reggie Neal's father Leonard had the Old Stores further down Shop Street from 1934 and Reggie began trading at Vine House (pictured above) in the early1950s until about 1981. The van below was a familiar sight for many years, serving the villagers within a six mile radius, delivering groceries, etc. from dawn until dusk.

134. Whatever you want, I will get it for you. Seeds to sausages, buttons to beer, bread to batteries, watches to whisky, ham to hammers. Reggie Neal loved a good deal!!

135. Bessie and Roy Elmy Gobbitt with Mr. and Mrs. Arthur Baldwin at St. Mary's church on the occasion of Ray Mayhew's wedding in 1964.

136. Stanley Mayhew and possibly Alan Smith stand on the forecourt of Worlingworth garage in 1966. An iconic photograph of a Smiths of Worlingworth van!

137. Caroline and Frank Newson celebrate their Golden Wedding anniversary in 1966. Frank was Worlingworth's last sexton.

138. Frank and Caroline Newson greet Reverend Bill Donnan and his wife Joyce at the entrance to St. Mary's church.

Page 102

139. June Abbott, Bruce Hill, Herbie Palfrey, Digger Turnbull and Charlie Abbott form the working party enjoying a snack at Worlingworth church in 1970.

140. "Robin Hood" with Mr. Piper at Worlingworth Primary School in 1972. Details with childrens names are given in the appendices.

141. 1970s bell-ringers at St. Mary's church. Left to right: George Hill, Herbie Palfrey, Harold Leathers, Alfred Chapman, Gerald Rumsey, Stanley Hawes, Clayton Hill and Harry Baldry.

142. Pictured here in the late 1970s are the "Three Rogues" - Reverend Bill Donnan, and brothers Clayton and Bruce Hill of Carters Farm, Water Lane.

143. This image from the late 1970s shows David and Sylvia Tye in front of their shop with their competition-winning prize washing machine.

144. At the wedding of Norman and Susan Saunders at St. Lawrence's church, Brundish on October 21st 1978, one of the photographs taken was this portrait of the five Crowe sisters, all daughters of Tom Crowe, the former landlord of the Swan Inn. From left to right is Betty Threadkell, Brenda Tuckwell, Hazel Eaton, Audrey Palfrey and Maisie Tuckwell.

145. The inaugural fete on the new playing field in 1979 was opened by Christine Webber from Anglia TV. Here she is pictured surrounded by many of the youngsters.

146. The tug-of-war featured Joe Nightingale at one end, next to him Richard Kerry, and front Melvyn Harsent. Other people you may recognize are Ethel Greenard, Sally Bridges, Sheila Catling, Eileen Catling, David Ruffles, Joan and Ivan Neal, Dick and Shirley Goode, John Gobbitt, Roger Gobbitt and Jane Smith.

147. Joe Lawes and his engine at an early May Day Fete on Worlingworth Playing Field. The old pavilion can be seen in the background to the right.

148. Reggie Denny of Beecrofts Farm felting an outbuilding at the Worlingworth Rectory in 1981, home of Canon and Mrs. William Donnan.

149. In 1983 at the first Worlingworth Flower and Produce Show held after 55 years, Mr. Bruce Hill (Best Kept Garden) and Mrs. Janet Rodwell (Overall Champion) receive their trophies with sponsors Ian Lochhead and Chris and Stella Watson.

150. This family photograph was taken at the 1987 Golden Wedding celebration party of Norton Riley and Marguerite Whatling (both seated). From left to right standing are Walter "Font" Whatling, Leonard and Una (Babs) Woods, Nora and George Whatling.

151. Worlingworth Football Club with manager Ron Willetts (back row right). Players names are given in the appendices at the back of the book.

Page 110

152. Harold Kerry originally worked as a mechanic at various garages including Smith's Garage, Shop Street and JGH at Gobbitts Yard. This photograph taken in 2000 celebrates his first year in business at Saxtead Vehicle Services.

153. Ronnie Chambers will be especially remembered for "Ron's Relics", his extensive collection of bygones which he would display at Worlingworth fetes and church fund-raisers.

154. Mr. Tony Fairweather was the village postman for twenty-five years and was awarded the Jubilee Cup for his long service in 1995.

155. Mr. David Tye with Geoff Hubbard's horse Trader Tye in the early 1990s.

156. Messrs. Herbie Palfrey, Harry Baldry, the Rev. John Mincher and Mrs. Joyce Canfer organising the raffle at the Church Christmas Bazaar held at the Community Centre in November 1995.

157. Dr. Brian Goodge being presented with a cheque on his retirement from medical practice in Stradbroke and the surrounding area in June 1997.

158. Worlingworth Cricket Club 1st XI possibly in 1995. From the top left: Doug Ramsey, Roger Gobbitt, Tom Giles, Phil Cantrell, Adrian Whatling, Kevin Wright. Front row: Harry Harper, Robert Nesling, Chris Watson, Geoffrey Robinson and Derek Cook.

159. The forecourt of Smith's Garage on Shop Street, now the site of Smith's Close.

160. Elizabeth and Ian Lochhead of the Red House cut the cake at their farewell party before leaving for Malta in 1999. Ian McKechnie (left) and the Reverend David Streeter (right) look on. Elizabeth held a Sunday School on a Friday at her home.

161. Paul Whatling, master thatcher of Beecroft's Farm, hosing down the thatching straw.

162. This is a once-in-a-lifetime photograph of Haley Chittock, Peggy Calver, Tracy Wright, Amanda Richards, Tracey Freeman and standing below Ann Bickers, known as the Millennium Girls, who had the idea of a new village sign and bench for which they raised the money. Pictured here before the unveiling in 2000.

163. Shirley Rutterford, Digger Turnbull and Pat Kench in the nave of the church in 2002, with the 1810 King George III Jubilee Feast painting in the background. The painting was to be restored with the help of an award from the Woodmansterne Trust. (EADT)

164. In 2004, churchwarden emeritus of St. Mary's church Herbie Palfrey received a long service award from the Diocese of St. Edmundsbury.

165. Stanley Hawes being presented with the Jubilee Cup by Chairman of the Parish Council Rosemary Ingate in 2004 at the Pet Service at Mill Farm. The award was given in recognition of his church fund-raising, including the Suffolk Historic Churches Trust Cycle Rides.

166. Major Bill Stringer of The Old Stores, Shop Street, and formerly of the Royal Horse Guards, is pictured in his garden on the occasion of Remembrance Day on Sunday November 9th 2008. He laid the wreath of poppies at the War Memorial and read out the names of the fallen.

167. Mrs. Janet Rodwell receiving the new Jubilee Cup from Mr. Keith Wilson at the 2011 Flower and Produce Show, in recognition of her support of St. Mary's church. Mrs. Eileen Catling is holding the original Silver Jubilee Cup dating from 1977.

168. Pam, Bernie and Steven Bickers working at "Steve's Plants" nursery in 2012.

169. Celebrating the first Worlingworth book of photographs, this lovely cake was made by Mrs. Veronica Plowman and was the centre-piece of a table display at the book launch. This photograph was taken by Robert Shepperson.

170. Robert Shepperson will always be remembered for dashing up and down the main street on his bicycle. Robert was a fine artist and photographer and he contributed greatly to the Village Record and the Worlingworth Parish Plan. The Worlingworth Wayfinder footpaths map is vividly illustrated with his colourful wildlife drawings, which are a testament to the many hours he spent walking around the parish sketching. He exhibited his fine art work at many local exhibitions.

171 and 172. Celebrating the Queen's Diamond Jubilee at the Community Centre in 2012 with Worlingworth's very own King and Queen, John Smith and Betty Beecroft. The sign, celebrating 35 years of the community's playing field, pavilion and present Community Centre, is being held by Rosemary Ingate, Keith Wilson and Betty Beecroft.

Page 124

173. Pat Kench and Nick Cook stand next to one of the entries for the inaugural Christmas Tree Festival in 2012. (Diss Express)

174. A recent photograph of Olive Larter taken at the front of the old Worlingworth Crown. Olive was the daughter of Charles Larter who was the occupier of the Crown on Fingal Street during the First World War.

175. Rena Iris Spurling (1916-2015), featured earlier in the book, lived to the grand old age of 99 years and held many wonderful memories of a very happy life at the Crown in Fingal Street in Worlingworth.

176. Sheila Heffer began working at the primary school in the canteen in 1967 and dedicated 46 years of her life to feeding the schoolchildren. She retired in July 2013 and was awarded the Jubilee Cup in that year. (EADT)

177. The children of Worlingworth Primary School take a break from rehearsals for the 2015 Nativity play. The most recent OFSTED report for the school rated all aspects of the school's work as "outstanding", an achievement to be proud of.

178. A recent feature of village fund-raising has been the annual opening to the public of a wildflower meadow at Barton Grange. In 2013, the Wildflower Meadow Weekend was featured on a television series about bee-keeping, presented by Martha Kearney. Pictured here with Martha are event organisers Matthew Hicks and Nick Cook. (EADT)

179. The community around the parish church used to gather on a regular basis to enjoy the hospitality of Mrs. Audrey Lewis of White Lea. In this photograph, Audrey's 90th birthday is being celebrated in December 2015.

180. Fred Uff completed the London Marathon in 2007 at the age of 73, raising £1,000 for the development of the play area at the Community Centre. So it was fitting that Fred cut the ribbon at the opening ceremony in July 2013. (EADT)

181. The Swan Inn entrance and seating area. A visual memory. (EADT)

182. The Worlingworth Swan has been providing a warm welcome and refreshment to residents and travellers alike for over four hundred years. In 2016 the prospect of our village inn closing down for ever has become an increasing possibility. We can only hope that, in the near future, this historic village asset's viability is secured. (EADT)

# ACKNOWLEDGEMENTS

Many of the photographs reproduced in the previous pages are held in the village archives. However, this book would not have been possible without the contributions of residents and also by those who live elsewhere but who have close family ties to the parish.

The authors would like to sincerely thank all those people for their generous contributions of photographs to this publication. We would like to acknowledge the contributions made by the following individuals and organisations:

| | |
|---|---|
| Charlie Abbott | Jan Ackroyd |
| Betty Beecroft | Pam Bickers |
| Jean Brett | David Bridges |
| Dawn Cape | Eileen Catling |
| George Chambers | Amy Chapman |
| Verdun Chapman | Daphne Clarke |
| Pam Ellemor | Shirley Fall |
| John Firth | Leonora Gane |
| Anna Goodge | Stephen Govier |
| Sara Hartest | Gerald Hawes |
| Nora Ingate | Stephen Ling |
| Ray Mayhew | Edna Meggs |
| Mary Nightingale | Daphne Neal |
| Elizabeth Owen | Janet Rodwell |
| Peggy Ruscoe | Pam Sanderson |
| Wendy Shepperson | Stephen Spandl |
| Brian Spurling | Cecile Stafford |
| David Steel | Robin Trembath |
| David Tye | Margaret Underwood |
| Brian Whatling | Paul Whatling |

Jean, Marion and Patricia Whiting

Diss Express
East Anglian Daily Times
Pettaugh History Society
Suffolk Records Office
Worlingworth Local History Group
Worlingworth Primary School

We would also like to thank everyone who made photographic contributions which we have been unable to include in this publication.

Every effort has been made to ensure that, to the best of our knowledge, the information in the picture captions is correct. We accept contributions and the accompanying descriptions in good faith. The editor apologises in advance for any errors or omissions.

# APPENDICES

## ADDITIONAL NOTES ON THE PHOTOGRAPHIC IMAGES

**Pictures 1 & 2:** The 4th Lord Henniker was responsible for the appointment of Frederic French as rector in 1853. These first images are not photographs but they are relevant in the context of the history of Worlingworth and merit inclusion on that basis.

**Picture 3:** The Hennikers never permanently lived at Worlingworth Hall. It was used mainly as a weekend retreat for relaxation, riding and shooting. The 5th Lord and his family used the Hall quite frequently during the 1870s.

**Picture 24:** Originally it was thought that it was the Parish Fire Engine that was standing in view of the cameraman (John Self of Framlingham) but closer inspection proved that this was not the case.

**Picture 49:** If the registration number of the car had been visible, the registered owner could be determined by looking at the motor vehicle registration ledgers at the Suffolk Records Office. Miss Dolly Tate of Stradbroke, organist, was a participant in a number of church events at Worlingworth and she would have been well-acquainted with the French family.

**Picture 64:** The Hawes family moved from Southolt to Lodge Farm, Worlingworth in 1919. Back row from left to right: Harry, Hubert, Stanley, Nellie, Robert and below Arthur and Elizabeth Hawes and Edward, John seated at the front. Harry was the father of Amy, Stanley and Gerald Hawes.

**Picture 119:** Southolt Plough Darts Outing in 1955. Some attendees have been tentatively identified. Mostly surnames are given starting at the top, from left to right and continuing in that vein:
Mr and Mrs Crane, Mr and Mrs Jolly; Whatling, Flatt, Fisk, Grey;
Pleasance, Smith, ?, ?, List, Whiting, Lawes, "Slobs" Archer; Lister;
Three unknowns, Whayman, Cuthbert, Hart, Lawes, Tate;
Bickers, Bickers, Cuthbert, Stone (landlord), Mrs Stone, son Stone, Flatt, Muttock, Bloss.

**Picture 121:** Worlingworth Juniors football team in the 1950s.
From left to right, back row: Mr. Spanton (teacher), David Goodchild, David Havers, Barry ?, Johnny Gobbitt, Fred Elliott;
Front row: Unknown, Ellis Farrington, Brian Whatling, Geoff Cuthbert, Ned Cuthbert, Peter Whatling.

# APPENDICES

ADDITIONAL NOTES ON THE PHOTOGRAPHIC IMAGES

**Picture 140:** "Robin Hood" at Worlingworth Primary School with Mr. Piper, headmaster in 1972.

Back row (left to right): Sheila Catling, Carol Elliott, Teresa Durrant, (face unseen:no ID), Gillian Nightingale, Mr. Leslie Piper, John Saxton (crown), Geoffrey Gobbitt (brown hat).

Front row (left to right): David Webster (spear), Paul Maybury (sword), Enid Hawes, Nicky Palfrey (sword), David Ruffles (spear), Sandra Ruffles (basket), Anthony Kemp (fur hat), Stephen Hawes (cape), Alex Negus (waistcoat), Alan Mayhew (bow), David Westrup (arrows), Tim Beecroft (hatchet).

**Picture 151:** Worlingworth Football Club in about 1988.

Back row: Karl Baldry, Tim Beecroft, Graham Biggs, Steven Biggs, Tony Palfreyman, David Webster, Geoff Gobbitt, Ron Willetts.

Front row: Jason Gobbitt, Ali Forster, Alan Jeffery, Roger Gobbitt, Roger Mayhew, Mark Rodwell.

# A History of the Worlingworth Swan

## Introduction
Much is made of the 20th century character of the Swan public house with its step-dancing tradition, horse fairs and warm Christmas welcomes by such landlords as Tom Crowe in the 1930s. But its earlier history could also be said to be vivid and full of the character befitting a traditional Suffolk agricultural wayside inn.

## History
An early reference to the inn is derived from the 1605 map of the manor of Worlingworth, where the building is clearly illustrated. The possible owner/occupier may have been a John Mayhew.

In the first Worlingworth Town Book, a 1714 entry names John Blaxall as the landlord. During the 18th century, the Ray family had ownership of the inn, along with their malting business further up Shop Street. Oliver Crouch appears to have been the landlord in the second half of the century.

The history of the establishment comes into focus at the time of the French Revolution and the Napoleonic Wars. Robert Chaplin was the landlord when the historic first committee meeting of the Loyal Worlingworth Volunteers took place on May 15th 1798 attended by no less a person than John Henniker-Major, the future 2nd Lord Henniker.

At this time the inn was the community centre of its time. It was renowned locally for its bowling green, where bowls, quoits, prize-fighting and even gurning through a horse's collar were popular and amusing pursuits. It was the venue of many tithe dinners, auctions and harvest horkey celebrations. It was where the fire brigade would slake their thirst after the annual exercising of the parish fire engine and it was where owners of well-bred Suffolk horses would bring their stallions to be covered in the early spring.

More than anything else, it was a place where the labourers and craftsmen could socialise with each other and discuss the issues of the day without any interruption. It also claimed most of the men's wages to the detriment of their families.

A more sombre use was made of the premises from time to time when inquests were held to determine the cause of a sudden or unusual death. The body of the deceased would be kept on the premises, probably underneath the floor of the landing upstairs - the coolest place - and then laid out on a table during the proceedings. An inquest was a notable event for the parish and the inn would do very good business that day.

There were many interesting landlords (and landladies) in the 19th century. The landlord would probably have had a second trade which he would carry out in an adjacent building or barn e.g. as a wheelwright, blacksmith or carpenter. His wife would look after the clientele.

Michael Spurling was landlord at the time of the 1810 Golden Jubilee Feast when he was reimbursed £32 for the supply of beer to between 4,000 and 5,000 visitors to Worlingworth Hall. This equates to about 600-700 gallons of beer produced—a lengthy process.

After Spurling's death in 1831, the inn was bought by the Cobbold Brewery and William Kemp, from a local family, became the landlord. The Kemps were Brundish blacksmiths who managed a number of the local hostelries such as the Horseshoes at Tannington. After Kemp, for a short time came an immigrant from London - Julius Cavalli.

By 1850, another local family became the licensees - the Newsons. James Newson was described as a wheelwright and victualler in 1855. His daughter Phyllis married Garneys Pattle (another unusual name), a journeyman harnessmaker from Wymondham, Norfolk. When Newson became the workhouse superintendent at the Hoxne Union Workhouse in 1861, Pattle became the licensee of the Swan.

Pattle and his wife ran a fairly tight establishment. There were a number of Petty Session cases where some of the more unruly patrons of the inn were prosecuted for drunkenness or disorder offences. Pattle's daughter Kate married William Greenard in 1867 and they moved to Easton where Greenard became the landlord of the White Horse. A resident of "Latchings" on Swan Road, Barney Greenard, can today trace his ancestry back to Garneys Pattle.

Pattle met an unfortunate end when he took his own life by hanging himself in a now-demolished barn at the Swan Inn in August 1881. His corpse may well have been laid out on a table that he would have dined at. His wife Phyllis took over the running of the Swan for a few years, eventually marrying Joseph Leggett in 1885. This partnership continued until the mid-1890s when first Joseph and then Phyllis succumbed to old age.

The following fifty years to the end of the Second World War probably represent the period when the bowling green was in its prime condition and the Worlingworth Bowls Club were a match for any team in the district. Local newspapers are replete with descriptions of "excellent matches" and a "capital repast" put on afterwards by "mine host" when toasts and singing entertained all. George Thurston, and father and son Frederick and Tom Crowe are worthy of mention in that respect.

Of course, as agriculture suffered so many downturns over the years, the pub trade suffered likewise. For a period during the 1970s, the property deteriorated to such a point that some customers recall supping their beer whilst rainwater dripped onto them through the leaking roof and yet the Swan Inn has always managed to survive these crises and downturns. Its popularity has remained high with its regulars and seasonal travellers alike. It is still very much a public house "in the Suffolk tradition."

# Chronology of Worlingworth

~650 – Place-name "Wilrincgawerda". Early field name "Wallhill".

~1035 – King Cnut gave Worlingworth to Bishop Aelfric who gave it to Bury St. Edmunds.

1086 – Domesday Book. Population unfree ~140.

~1100 – Free tenants established.

~1250 – Population surge after rise in agricultural productivity. Green is established.

1250 – First manorial documents. Manor Farm in block of crofts at east end of village.

~1300 – Feudal system and population is at its peak.

1315-1318 – Great famine.

1327 – Tax returns for Worlingworth suggest one of poorest villages in Suffolk. Population 482?

1349 - Black Death. ~40% of people die in 6 months. House sites become abandoned.

1361 – Second pestilence. ~15% die. Government price controls resisted in inns.

1381 – Peasants Revolt. Passive rebellion in Worlingworth. Long term effects on agriculture.

1391 – Murder of John Farman by Roger Clerke and John Swon.

1466 – Survey of manor links later documents to medieval archive. 90 tenements.

1474 – 1st bequest to Worlingworth Town Lands Charity.

1536 – Reformation. Dissolution of smaller monasteries (Eye, Redlingfield, etc).

1538 – Parishes responsible for registration of baptisms, marriages and burials.

1539 – Dissolution of larger monasteries incl. Bury. Worlingworth sold to Anthony Rous. Guild of the Holy Trinity and Blessed Mary also dissolved.

1550 – Swan Inn newly built. Inn previously on the other side of Swan "Lane".

1558 – Worlingworth parish registers begin. Pest-house on Great Green.

~1606 – First map of Worlingworth.

1643 – Dowsing's Journal. Desecration of Worlingworth church.

1665-6 – Great Plague. Worlingworth largely escaped, unlike Framlingham and Woodbridge.

1689 – John Baldry's Charity is established, including the teaching of grammar.

1698 – William Godbold's Charity enhances Baldry's educational bequest.

1730 – Series of parish maps drawn.

1739 – The old Guildhall is opened as a Parish Poorhouse.

1760 – Parish Fire Engine given by John Major.

1768 – William Ray, Gent, of the Red House expires in Norwich marketplace.

1780 – The Rectory is rebuilt.

1781 – Sir John Major dies. He is interred in the chancel of the church.

1784 – Registers record that Edward Rivers "drowned in a fit of lunacy".

1790 – William Ray Jnr., found dead in a hackney coach, crossing Blackfriars Bridge in London.

1798 – Worlingworth Loyal Volunteers militia formed.

1799 – Charles Farmery founded the Baptist Church at Horham.

1801 – First National Census. Pop. 653. Napoleonic War makes arable farming very profitable.

1808 – Three cases of typhus fever recorded in the Parish Poorhouse.

1810 – The Worlingworth Jubilee Feast in commemoration of George III's 50 year reign.

1815—Samuel Ray, dealer, malster, merchant and chapman, is declared a bankrupt.

1816 – Peace returns to Europe. Farm profits decline. Unemployment brings migration & emigration.

1818 – School erected to the east of church.

1825 – Schoolmaster's house is added.

1829—Cricket on Worlingworth Green between the Worlingworth "club" and Eye.

1831-2 – Enclosure of Worlingworth Green.

1833 – Malicious fires at farms along Shop Street and Southolt Road.

1834 - Stradbroke Union Workhouse is opened for the Hoxne Hundred.

1836 – The Parish Poorhouse is closed and the furniture and effects auctioned off at the Swan Inn.

1837 – Worlingworth Tithe Map drawn up.

1849 - A great April snowstorm hit Suffolk, causing stagecoaches to be buried in snow drifts.

1851 – "Great" National Census. Population 811. Migration to work in towns and cities gathers pace.

1853 - Inauguration of Reverend Frederic French as Rector in October.

1859 – First revived Harvest Home celebration.

1865 – Major cattle plague outbreak.

1866 – Church restoration begun, significant changes to the chancel.

1872 - John Clayton, parish clerk for 48 years, dies, leaving 10 children, 43 grandchildren and 45 great grandchildren.

1873 – Several families in Fingal Street migrate to the cotton mills of Lancashire.

1876—Worlingworth Brass Band formed by Samuel Collins.

1876 – New School opened on land given by William Godbold.

1879 – First Worlingworth Cart Colt Show.

1886 – Three cottages near Mill Farm destroyed by fire.

1887 – Golden Jubilee Feast in commemoration of Queen Victoria's 50 year reign.

1888 – Village library is opened.

1889 – James Newson, carpenter, dies in his 100th year.

1890 – First annual Worlingworth & Southolt Flower & Produce Show.

1891 – Census. Population 574. Agriculture emerging from depression?

1892 – Major influenza epidemic in first two months of the year.

1895 – Parish Council formed. Alfred Preston is the first chairman.

1897 – Diamond Jubilee Feast in commemoration of Queen Victoria's 60 year reign.

1898 – Telegraph comes to Worlingworth.

1901 – 1,025 burials in the churchyard during the previous 100 years.

1907 – Death of Frederic French, 54 years Rector of Worlingworth.

1908 – Worlingworth Station opened. Excursion to Felixstowe 3s 3d.

1915 – Major William Cotton French of 3rd Gurkhas killed in action at Neuve Chapelle.

1918 – Auction of Henniker estates situated in and around Worlingworth.

1921 – Isabel Foster, former landlady of the Swan Inn, found drowned near Paradise Farm.

1922 – Victory Hall, the new community hall, is established near the school.

1935—Worlingworth Football Club's first competitive fixture versus Framlingham Town.

1940 – P.C. Ernest Whiting and five engineers killed by an unexploded bomb on Fingal Street.

1948 – Auction of remaining Henniker properties in Worlingworth.

1950 – Worlingworth Mill dismantled.

1951—Death of Reverend George T. Wilkes, Rector of Worlingworth.

1952 – Mid-Suffolk Light Railway closes.

1968 – Jim Kemp, the last Worlingworth blacksmith, dies aged 84.

1976 – Frank Newson, former sexton, dies aged 85.

1977—Worlingworth Jubilee Cup inaugurated for community service.

1979—First Worlingworth Fete on the new Community Field.

1981—A Community Pavilion is erected and opened on the Community Field.

1982—Worlingworth-cum-Southolt Annual Flower and Produce Show is re-established.

1992—The present Community Centre opens.

2000—Millenium celebrations and erection of a new village sign and bench.

2002 – Golden Jubilee Celebration at Worlingworth Hall.

2008—Completion of Worlingworth Footpaths Scheme.

2012—Diamond Jubilee Celebration and first Worlingworth book published.

2016—Queen's 90th Birthday celebrated on April 21st.